MULTICULTURAL SEASONAL CRAFTS

Winter Crafts from Different Cultures

12 Projects to Celebrate the Season

BY MEGAN BORGERT-SPANIOL

a Capstone company — publishers for children

Raintree is an imprint of Capstone Global Library Limited, a company incorporated in England and Wales having its registered office at 264 Banbury Road, Oxford, OX2 7DY – Registered company number: 6695582

www.raintree.co.uk
myorders@raintree.co.uk

Hardback edition © Capstone Global Library Limited 2023
Paperback edition © Capstone Global Library Limited 2024

The moral rights of the proprietor have been asserted. All rights reserved. No part of this publication may be reproduced in any form or by any means (including photocopying or storing it in any medium by electronic means and whether or not transiently or incidentally to some other use of this publication) without the written permission of the copyright owner, except in accordance with the provisions of the Copyright, Designs and Patents Act 1988 or under the terms of a licence issued by the Copyright Licensing Agency, 5th Floor, Shackleton House, 4 Battle Bridge Lane, London, SE1 2HX (www.cla.co.uk). Applications for the copyright owner's written permission should be addressed to the publisher.

British Library Cataloguing in Publication Data
A full catalogue record for this book is available from the British Library.

ISBN 978 1 3982 4538 9 (hardback)
ISBN 978 1 3982 4537 2 (paperback)

Editorial Credits
Editor: Jessica Rusick
Designer: Sarah DeYoung
Originated by Capstone Global Library Ltd

Image Credits
Project and materials photos: Mighty Media, Inc.; Shutterstock: Djomas, 10 (child)

Design Elements
Shutterstock: KALYA MALYA, lukeruk, sherilhome

All the internet addresses (URLs) given in this book were valid at the time of going to press. However, due to the dynamic nature of the internet, some addresses may have changed, or sites may have changed or ceased to exist since publication. While the author and publisher regret any inconvenience this may cause readers, no responsibility for any such changes can be accepted by either the author or the publisher.

CONTENTS

Winter 4

Hanukkah 6

Winter Solstice 8

Seasonal craft 10

Kwanzaa 12

New Year's Eve 14

Lohri 16

New Year 18

Valentine's Day 20

Chinese New Year 22

Mardi Gras 24

Seasonal craft 26

Christmas 28

   Find out more 32

   About the author 32

Winter

What is your favourite part of winter? Is it the snowy evergreen trees or cosy hats and scarves? Maybe it's all the seasonal celebrations, including Hanukkah, Valentine's Day and Chinese New Year!

Celebrate winter with cool projects that reflect the season. Create your own cork Kwanzaa candles or Black History bunting. You might even build a woollen bonfire for Lohri or an egg carton mask for Mardi Gras. Winter is filled with enough natural beauty and festivities to keep you crafting all season long!

BASIC SUPPLIES

balloons

cardboard

hot glue gun

paint and paintbrushes

ruler

scissors

tape

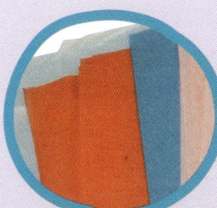
tissue paper

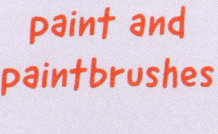
toothpicks

string

CRAFTING TIPS

Be prepared! Read through the materials and instructions before starting a project. Cover your workspace with paper or plastic to protect it from messes or spills.

Think outside the book! Lots of the projects in this book use materials you'll probably find around your home. Is there something you can't find? Think of ways to adapt the project using items you do have.

Ask first! Get permission before using materials you find at home or school. Also, ask before you collect items from nature and bring them indoors.

Be safe! Ask an adult for help with projects that require sharp or hot tools.

Clean up! When your project is complete, put all materials and tools back where you found them. Clean up any spills and wipe down your crafting surface.

HANUKKAH
Marshmallow dreidels

A dreidel is a spinning top with four sides. Each side shows a different Hebrew letter. It's a tradition to play with a dreidel on Hanukkah, a Jewish celebration lasting eight days. Make your own edible dreidels using marshmallows, chocolates and pretzels!

Fun fact
During Hanukkah, families tell a story from the Talmud, a Jewish text. The story tells of candles that burned for eight nights on only a small amount of oil.

What you need

- 250 g white chocolate chips
- measuring cup
- microwave
- microwave-safe bowl
- spatula
- blue food colouring
- small pretzel sticks
- large marshmallows
- spoon
- Hershey's Kisses (or chocolate cut into triangle shape)
- baking tray
- greaseproof paper
- sprinkles (optional)

What you do

1. Pour the white chocolate chips into a microwave-safe bowl.

2. Microwave the chips 30 seconds at a time, stirring between each round, until the chips are melted. Stir in blue food colouring until the mixture is uniformly coloured.

3. Push a small pretzel stick into one end of each marshmallow.

4. Dip the marshmallow into the blue chocolate. Use a spoon to smooth out the chocolate on the marshmallow. Work quickly, as the chocolate will start to harden.

5. Stick the flat end of a Hershey's Kiss to the end of the marshmallow opposite the pretzel.

6. Lay the dreidel on a baking tray lined with greaseproof paper. Use sprinkles to decorate the dreidel if you like.

7. Repeat steps 4 to 5 to make more dreidels.

8. Refrigerate the tray of dreidels for about 30 minutes. Then enjoy your treat!

WINTER SOLSTICE
Ice luminary

In the northern hemisphere, winter solstice takes place in December and marks the first day of winter. This day has the fewest hours of sunlight in the year. In many countries, people mark the winter solstice by lighting candles. Celebrate the solstice by creating a beautiful ice luminary to light up the night!

What you need

- duct tape
- large tin
- large plastic container
- dried beans, marbles or rocks
- water
- red berries, pine cones and winter greenery (real or fake)
- freezer
- LED tea light

What you do

1. Stick four strips of duct tape around the edge of the tin. Place the tin inside the plastic container so their rims are level. Attach the other ends of the tape strips to the container's rim.

2. Fill the tin with dried beans, marbles or rocks. Pour water between the tin and plastic container, leaving an inch or two of space at the top.

3. Place red berries, small pine cones and winter greenery into the water around the tin.

4. Place the plastic container in a freezer. Let the water freeze.

5. Remove the material from the inside of the tin. Fill the tin with hot water to help release it from the ice. Also run hot water around the outside of the plastic container.

6. Place an LED tea light into your ice luminary. Store in a freezer if needed. Display the luminary outdoors!

SEASONAL CRAFT

Cosy checked scarf

Scarves keep our necks warm both indoors and out. These popular accessories are often made by sewing or knitting. But you can make your own cosy scarf using just an old checked shirt and some hot glue!

What you need

- old long-sleeve checked shirt
- fabric scissors
- marker pen
- hot glue gun

What you do

1. Cut the arms off the shirt at the shoulder.

2. Open up the sleeves by making one cut down the length of each one.

3. Lay the body of the shirt flat so the back side faces up. Lay one open sleeve flat over the back. Use a marker to trace the sleeve piece.

4. Cut out the shape you traced from the back of the shirt.

5. Place the three sleeve shapes side by side so their short ends meet.

6. Spread hot glue along one short edge of the middle piece. Fold under the edge of the side piece and place the folded part on top of the line of glue. This creates a clean seam.

7. Repeat step 6 to connect the second side piece to the middle piece.

8. Flip the scarf over. Use hot glue to connect the long edges of the sleeves in clean seams. Now your cosy scarf is ready to wear!

KWANZAA
Cork Kwanzaa candles

Kwanzaa is a seven-day celebration of African heritage and culture. An important symbol of Kwanzaa is the kinara, a candleholder for seven candlesticks. A new candle is lit each night of Kwanzaa. Make your own kinara and candles out of wood, cork bottle stoppers and some paint!

Fun fact

All families have their own ways of lighting Kwanzaa candles. One common tradition is to light the black candle on the first night. The remaining candles are lit from left to right (red then green) over the following nights.

What you need

- 7 cork bottle stoppers
- paint (red, green black, optional colour of your choice) and paintbrushes
- 30-centimetre (12-inch) narrow block of wood
- hot glue gun
- orange and yellow tissue paper
- scissors
- toothpick
- sewing pins

What you do

1. Paint three corks red, three green and one black. Let the paint dry.

2. If you like, you can paint the block of wood a colour of your choosing. Let it dry.

3. Lay the block of wood flat. Glue the black cork upright in the middle of the block's length.

4. Glue the red corks upright to the left of the black cork. Glue the green corks upright to the right of the black cork.

5. Wrap squares of orange and yellow tissue paper around the end of a toothpick, creating a flame.

6. To "light" a candle, use a straight pin to attach the flame to the top of a cork.

7. Add a new flame to the set of candles each night of Kwanzaa!

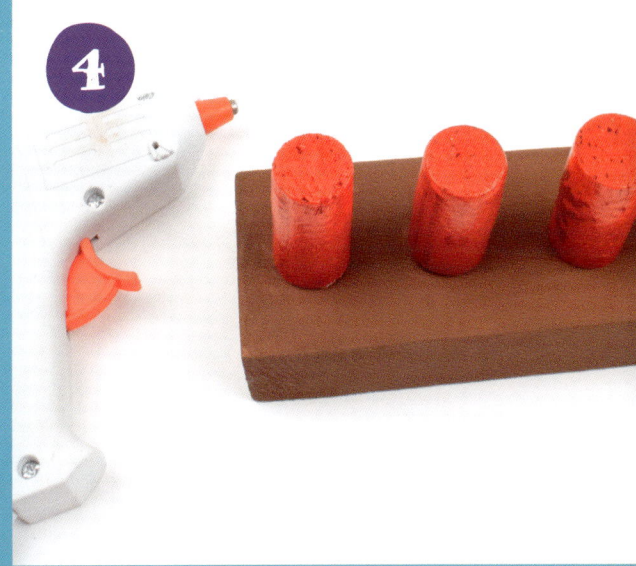

NEW YEAR'S EVE
Confetti popper

On 31 December, millions of people across the world stay up late to ring in the new year. At midnight, skies erupt with fireworks and people cheer and wish each other a Happy New Year. Make a homemade confetti popper for your own New Year's celebration!

Fun fact

In Scotland, New Year's Eve is called Hogmanay. It is the most important Scottish holiday of the year. People celebrate with fireworks, meals, music and dancing.

What you need

- balloon
- scissors
- cardboard tube (an empty toilet roll is the perfect size)
- packing tape
- wrapping paper or other decorative paper
- craft glue
- old magazines

What you do

1. Tie a knot in the neck of the balloon. Then cut off the very end of the rounded top.

2. Wrap the body of the balloon around one end of the cardboard tube. Secure the balloon in place with packing tape.

3. Cover the cardboard tube with wrapping paper or other decorative paper. Secure the paper with glue.

4. Cut colourful old magazine pages into confetti.

5. Fill the cardboard tube with confetti. Hold the tube in one hand and pull the balloon knot down with the other. Release the knot to send the confetti flying!

6. Remember to recycle your confetti and popper after the celebrations are over!

LOHRI
Glowing bonfire

Lohri is a harvest festival celebrated primarily in northern India. On this day, people build bonfires in honour of Agni, the Hindu god of fire. Popcorn, peanuts and other food are thrown into the fires as offerings. Build your own Lohri bonfire out of wooden skewers and wool!

What you need

- plastic lid with about a 12-centimetre (5-in) diameter
- craft knife
- 6 wooden skewers
- hot glue gun
- small elastic band
- yellow, orange and red wool
- scissors
- pebbles

What you do

1. Ask an adult to cut the rim off the lid to make a flat circle. Cut six equally-spaced holes around the lid's perimeter using a craft knife.

2. Stick one end of a wooden skewer through each small hole in the plastic lid. Use hot glue to secure each skewer.

3. Use a small elastic band to bind the other ends of the skewers. This forms a frame for your bonfire.

4. Tie yellow wool to the very top of the frame. Wrap the wool around the top third of the frame, hot gluing periodically. Cut the wool.

5. Tie orange wool to the loose end of the yellow wool. Wrap the orange wool around the middle third of the frame. Cut the wool.

6. Repeat step 5 to wrap the bottom third of the frame in red wool. Hot glue the end of the wool in place.

7. Hot glue pebbles onto the lid around the fire's base. Then display your bonfire!

NEW YEAR

To-do list wipe-clean board

The start of a new year brings a fresh list of to-dos and resolutions. Resolve to stay organised with your own funky wipe-clean board to show task lists, reminders or words of encouragement!

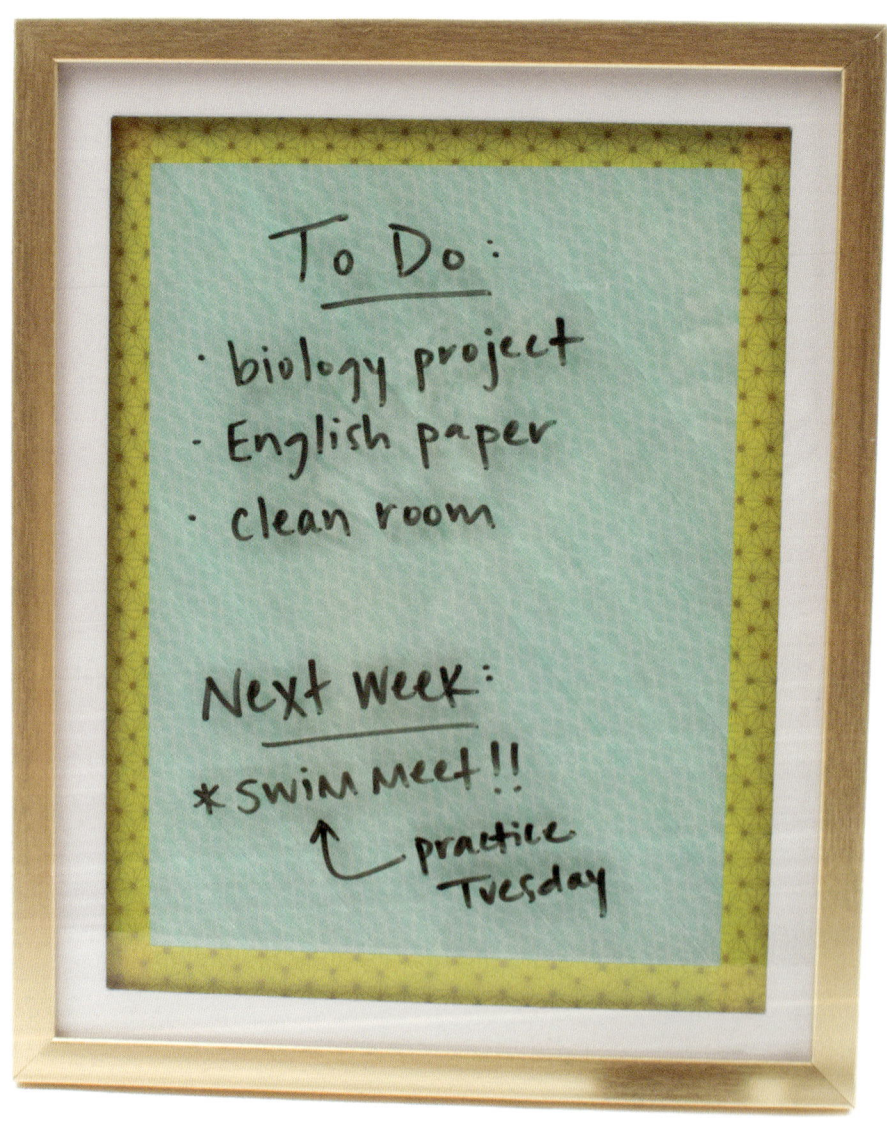

What you need

- picture frame
- paint and paintbrush (optional)
- scissors
- craft tape
- wipe-clean marker pen

What you do

1. Take the cardboard backing out of the frame. If you want to paint the frame, carefully take the glass or plastic out of the frame too. Replace it when the paint is dry.

2. Cover the piece of paper or cardboard that comes in the frame with craft tape. Use pale colours so the dry-erase pens will show on top of them.

3. Place the paper or cardboard back into the picture frame and secure the backing.

4. Use the wipe-clean pen to write messages on the glass or plastic of the picture frame!

VALENTINE'S DAY
Heart coasters

Valentine's Day is recognized in various countries as a day to show appreciation for loved ones. People often exchange cards, flowers, chocolates and other gifts. Make heart coasters for some festive décor. Or, give them to someone special!

What you need

- coloured card
- ruler
- pencil
- scissors
- cork tiles
- craft knife
- paint (white, colours of your choice) and paintbrushes
- craft tape
- stickers (optional)

What you do

1. Cut a square of card with 10-cm (4-in) sides. Fold the square in half.

2. Starting and ending at the fold, cut half a heart out of the folded card.

3. Unfold the card to reveal a full heart.

4. Trace the heart on a cork tile. Ask an adult to help you cut out the heart from the cork using a craft knife.

5. Paint the top and sides of the cork heart white. Let the paint dry.

6. Use strips of craft tape to make a design on the heart.

7. Paint the different sections created by the tape using colours of your choice. Let the paint dry.

8. Pull the tape off the cork heart. It's ready to use as a coaster!

9. Repeat steps 4 to 7 to make more heart coasters. Try cutting the craft tape into thinner strips. You can also use stickers instead of tape to make designs on the cork!

CHINESE NEW YEAR

Chinese lantern

Chinese New Year begins with the new moon that occurs in January or February. For this reason, it is also known as Lunar New Year. To celebrate, people light fireworks, gather for meals and hang red lanterns. Make your own Chinese lantern to celebrate the Chinese New Year!

Fun fact

Red is a popular colour during Chinese New Year. It symbolizes good fortune and joy.

What you need

- red balloon
- red tissue paper
- ruler
- scissors
- bowl
- measuring cup
- white glue
- water
- paintbrush
- drinking glass
- black marker pen (optional)
- glitter glue (optional)
- hole punch
- string

What you do

1. Blow up the balloon and knot it.

2. Cut red tissue paper into strips 7.5 cm (3 in) long and 2.5 cm (1 in) wide.

3. In the bowl, mix together white glue and 120 ml (4 fl oz) water.

4. Brush some glue mixture onto part of the balloon. Cover the section with strips of tissue paper. Use the brush to smooth out the tissue paper on the balloon.

5. Repeat step 4 until the balloon is covered, except for the knot. Put the balloon in a drinking glass, knot side down. Let the tissue paper layer dry a bit.

6. Repeat steps 4 to 5 to add five or six layers to the balloon. Then let the lantern dry for 48 hours.

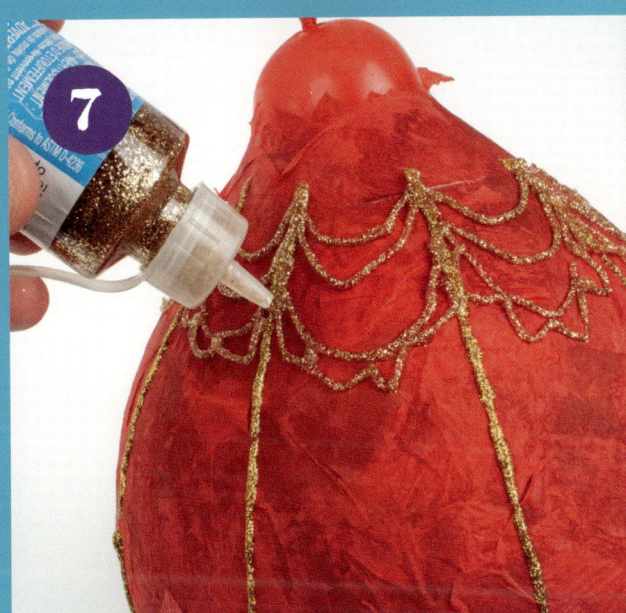

7. Decorate the lantern with black marker or glitter glue.

8. Cut off the balloon knot. Pull the balloon out of the lantern.

9. Punch a hole on either side of the lantern opening. Tie the ends of a long piece of string through the holes. Then hang your lantern!

MARDI GRAS
Jester mask

Mardi Gras is the day before the beginning of Lent, a Christian season of prayer and reflection. Mardi Gras celebrations are marked by lively parades and colourful costumes. Jester characters are a popular symbol of the festivities. Make your own jester mask with an egg box and some paint!

Fun fact

Mardi Gras means "Fat Tuesday" in French. Traditionally, it's a day of feasting before many Christians give up certain foods for Lent.

What you need

- empty egg box
- scissors
- craft knife
- paint (purple, green, gold) and paintbrushes
- wooden dowel
- decorative materials, such as pipe cleaners, bells, sequins and feathers
- hot glue gun

What you do

1. Cut two egg cups and the divider cone between them from the end of an empty egg box.

2. Ask an adult to use a craft knife to cut eyeholes in the egg cups.

3. Paint the mask purple, green and/or gold. Paint a thin wooden dowel using the same colours. Let everything dry.

4. Decorate the mask and dowel with pipe cleaners, bells, sequins, feathers or any other decorative materials you have.

5. Hot glue the dowel to the side of the mask. Hold the mask up to your face by holding the dowel!

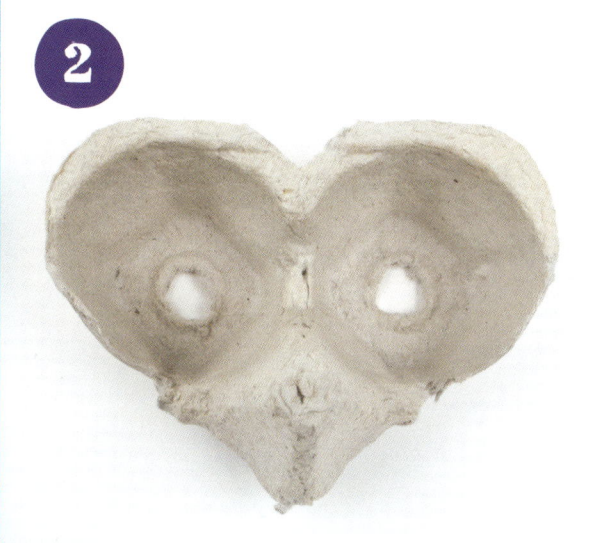

SEASONAL CRAFT

Mixed-media snowflake

When you look out at a blanket of fresh snow on the ground, what you're seeing is tiny frozen water crystals surrounded by air. Take a closer look at the crystals, and you'll discover some of the most intricate and delicate patterns nature has to offer. Celebrate the amazing snowflake with this mixed-media creation!

What you need

- paint (dark blue, light blue, white) and paintbrushes
- craft sticks
- clothes pegs
- toothpicks
- hot glue gun
- bead
- string

What you do

1. Paint four craft sticks dark blue. Let them dry.

2. Separate four clothes pegs into eight wood pieces. Paint the pieces light blue and let them dry.

3. Paint eight toothpicks white and let them dry.

4. Glue two craft sticks together to make a plus sign. Do the same with the other two. Glue the two pairs together into a snowflake.

5. Arrange the clothes peg pieces into a snowflake shape with their ends meeting in the centre. Glue the pieces together.

6. Glue the clothes peg snowflake on top of the craft stick snowflake.

7. Glue the toothpicks on top of the clothes peg snowflake so they align with the craft stick snowflake.

8. Glue a bead to the centre of the snowflake. Hang the snowflake with a loop of string!

CHRISTMAS

Festive gnome ornament

Christmas is a Christian holiday celebrating the birth of Jesus Christ. Many people celebrate Christmas by bringing a fir tree into their home and decorating it with ornaments. Make a cute gnome ornament to hang in your home!

What you need

- cardboard
- ruler
- scissors
- white wool
- felt
- marker pen
- hot glue gun
- large wooden bead
- small pom-pom
- puffy paint (optional)
- string

What you do

1. Cut a piece of cardboard that is 7.5 cm (3 in) wide and 10 cm (4 in) long.

2. Loosely wrap a length of white wool around the width of the cardboard piece about 60 times.

3. Slide the wool loop off the cardboard. Use another piece of wool to tie a knot around the middle of the wool loop.

4. Cut open the loops on either side of the knot you tied. This creates a pom-pom.

5. Trim the pom-pom so the wool is the same length all around.

6. Cut a triangle out of felt with two 11-cm (4¼-in) sides and one 16-cm (6¼-in) side.

7. Fold the triangle in half. Measure 7.5 cm (3 in) down the diagonal side of the triangle and make a mark.

8. Cut the folded triangle from the mark to the bottom edge.

9. Open up the triangle and cut to round out the bottom.

10. Overlap the sides of the triangle to form a cone hat. Use hot glue to create a seam where the felt overlaps.

11. Glue the hat on top of the pom-pom you made. Glue the wooden bead below the hat to make a nose.

12. Glue the small pom-pom to the top of the cone hat.

13. If you like, you can use puffy paint to decorate the hat in a festive pattern. Let it dry.

14. Cut a 25.5-cm (10-in) length of string. Knot the ends together to form a loop.

15. Glue the knot of the loop behind the top of the hat. Then hang your gnome up!

Fun fact

In Scandinavia, gnomes are part of Christmas tradition. Julenisse is a gnome said to bring presents to good children.

FIND OUT MORE

BOOKS

10-Minute Crafty Projects (10-Minute Makers), Elsie Olson (Raintree, 2022)

Black and British: An Illustrated History, David Olusoga (Macmillan Children's Books, 2021)

Celebrations Around the World (Customs Around the World), Wil Mara (Raintree, 2021)

WEBSITES

www.bbc.co.uk/cbbc/curations/bp-arts-and-crafts-collection
CBBC has lots of craft ideas you can make.

www.dkfindout.com/uk/more-find-out/festivals-and-holidays/chinese-new-year/
Learn about Chinese New Year with DKFindout!

ABOUT THE AUTHOR

Megan Borgert-Spaniol is an author and editor of children's media. When she isn't writing or reading, she enjoys doing yoga, eating croissants and making homemade pizzas. Megan lives in Minneapolis, Minnesota, USA, with a tall, goofy man and a small, chatty cat.